KIDS HAD JOBS
LIFE BEFORE CHILD LABOR LAWS

HISTORY BOOK FOR KIDS
CHILDREN'S HISTORY

BABY PROFESSOR
EDUCATION KIDS

Speedy Publishing LLC

40 E. Main St. #1156

Newark, DE 19711

www.speedypublishing.com

Copyright 2017

In this book, we're going to talk about life before child labor laws. So, let's get right to it!

During the Industrial Revolution, children from impoverished families often had to get jobs to contribute income to their households. It's difficult to believe this today, but children who were only four years of age were some of the youngest workers in factories. At that time, factories were very dangerous places.

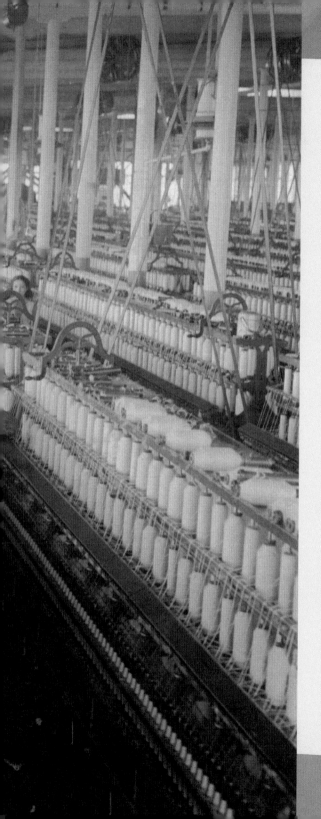

The machines in factories were new, but they hadn't always been tested for safety. The practice of using children for part of the labor force continued throughout the Industrial Revolution. Finally, in the 1900s, laws were passed to prevent young children from working long hours in unsafe conditions.

WHAT TYPES OF JOBS DID CHILDREN HAVE?

Children had all different types of jobs. They operated machines in factories and cleaned out chimneys. Sometimes employers preferred to hire kids instead of adults because they could squeeze into smaller spaces. There were three types of jobs that were very common—breaking up coal, creating matchsticks, and offering newspapers for sale on street corners.

BREAKER BOYS

Breaker boys had horrible jobs. They worked in the depths of the mines. The bulk of their jobs was to divide the huge hunks of coal as they traveled down conveyer belts. The coal had to be separated into equally sized chunks. It was also their job to take out anything that wasn't coal, such as soil, rocks, or clay. They had to do this by hand. The coal mine was dark and the air inside was toxic.

The breaker boys would sit all day, sometimes for 10 hours or more, on hard wooden stools to separate the coal pieces with their hands. They didn't have protective gloves and the sharp pieces inside the coal would wound their hands.

Over time, many had asthma or sometimes they developed cancer in their lungs and throats from the toxic dust in the mines. Other common injuries included the loss of limbs or fingers from the unsafe conveyor belts. Most breaker boys were between the ages of 8 and 12.

MATCHGIRLS

A majority of the workers laboring in the factories that produced matches were female and it was a common job for girls from ages 13 through 16. They were described as "matchgirls." One of the tasks in the factory was the step of creating the tips of the matches. In order to do this, they had to dip the sticks into a toxic chemical known as phosphorus.

The work was tedious, difficult, and dangerous. The young girls stood sometimes for 12 hours in succession and the wages were barely enough to buy food. If they didn't perform well, their employers would sometimes beat them for punishment. At times they had their fingers cut off by the machinery they were using.

The phosphorus was by far the deadliest part of their job. Breathing it caused illness and the chemical was so toxic that it broke down the enamel of their teeth and made their teeth fall out.

MATCHGIRL STRIKERS

NEWSIES

Newsies were some of the first child entrepreneurs. They were mostly orphan boys. They had to find some type of work to support themselves since they were living on the streets. Each child had his own business. They would buy newspapers each morning from the publishers. Then, they parked themselves on street corners.

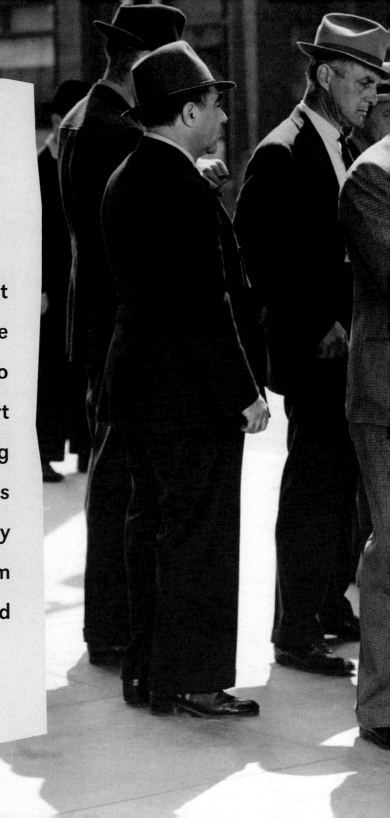

The corners with heavy street traffic were coveted. They called out to pedestrians to buy papers and sold as many as they could. If they sold all their papers, they would make a small profit and have enough to reinvest the following day. Sometimes if they didn't sell enough they lost money and couldn't eat.

In the year 1899, many publishers in the city of New York decided to increase their prices, which of course meant that the newsies had to pay higher prices too. The boys joined together and decided to strike. They did everything they could do to make it impossible for the publishers to sell their papers.

Finally, they brought the publishing management to their knees, and a compromise was worked out between the adult management and the young boys. The publishers didn't decrease their prices. However, they did agree to purchase any papers that the boys couldn't sell.

One of the kid strike leaders was named Kid Blink because he wore a patch over his blind eye. In those days, going without newspapers would be the same as stopping all television and internet today.

Kid Blink and the other kid leaders became some of the most powerful kids in history due to their bravery and their ability to get management to listen to their demands. The Walt Disney company created a movie about this real-life event in 1992 that was entitled "Newsies." In 2012, a musical about the Newsies was performed on Broadway and ran for over five years.

HOW MUCH MONEY DID CHILDREN RECEIVE FOR THEIR LABORS?

Another reason that employers preferred hiring child workers was because they didn't have to pay them as much as adults. Sometimes they didn't receive any pay at all, but were simply given shelter. If they were paid, it was generally at 10-20% of the amount that the adults were paid for the exact same task.

WHY DID THE BUSINESSES HIRE KIDS?

There were lots of reasons that employers decided to hire kids. They were inexpensive or free. They generally worked really hard and because of their size they could do some jobs that adults couldn't. Some employers who hired children treated them as if they were slaves.

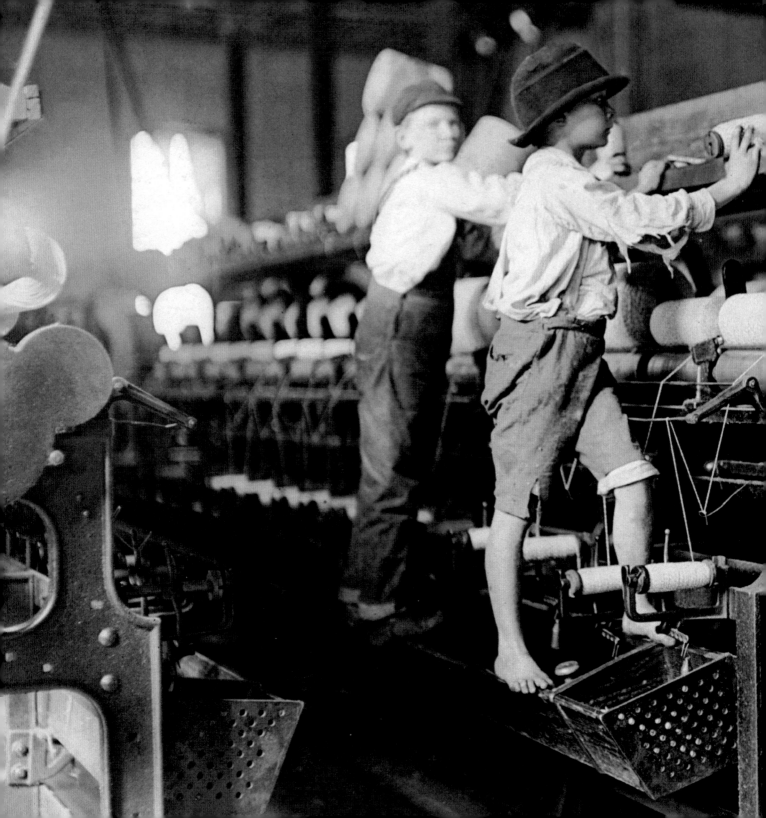

They were locked in their quarters and forced into working very long days. Other businesses hired kids because they knew there was a likelihood that they might starve on the streets if they weren't hired.

WHAT WERE THE WORKING CONDITIONS?

Many children died or were injured during the dangerous working conditions of the Industrial Revolution. There were almost no regulations or laws about protection from overwork or dangerous conditions. Many children weren't trained well on the machines they had to use so their fingers or limbs were cut off.

Those children that worked in the mines had some of the worst conditions of all. The air in the mines was toxic so over time they developed diseases in their lungs. At times they were subjected to unsafe chemicals and became very ill or died from the toxic fumes.

WAS CHILD LABOR A COMMON PRACTICE?

Child labor was very common throughout this era of history. In Britain, over half of the workers in factories at the start of the 1800s were 14 years of age or younger. In 1870 in the US, over 750,000 workers were less than 15 years of age.

AN END TO CHILD LABOR

One of the first laws regulating child labor was passed in Britain in 1833. This law made it illegal for children under 9 years of age to be hired. In the US, the government began to regulate child labor at the beginning of the 1900s. Many businesses opposed these regulations since their profits were dependent on hiring children.

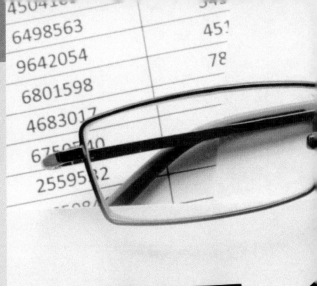

Some families were upset about the regulations too since they needed the income that the children earned. However, the government went forward to protect children and in 1938, a group of laws was passed called the Fair Labor Act. It provided limitations on the hiring of children, established a minimum wage, and also created limits for the number of hours for a standard workday.

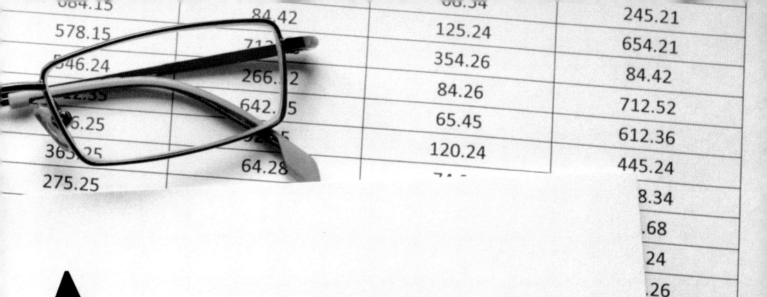

084.15		84.42		66.34	245.21
578.15		712	125.24		654.21
546.24		266. 2	354.26		84.42
42.35		642. 5	84.26		712.52
6.25			65.45		612.36
365 25			120.24		445.24
275.25		64.28			8.34

A

Standards Act

Children who were hired in the factories at an early age received little formal education.

Children without parents had to work or they would starve to death. Children who labored in coal mines often worked from 4 in the morning until 5 at night. The work was very harsh. Some of the children pulled coal wagons up underground tunnels all day back and forth. The tunnels were just a few feet in height.

CHILD MINE WORKERS

A photo taken by Lewis Hine showed the deplorable conditions of the Breaker Boys at a coal mine in Pennsylvania. It brought the situation to the public and helped the cause for child labor laws. In London, thousands of girls working in the match factories took to the streets in the year 1888 to protest their terrible working conditions.

TIMES WERE CHANGING

During the Industrial Revolution, children and teenagers represented over half of the labor force in Britain's factories at the beginning of the 1800s. In the United States in the 1870s over 750,000 children and teenagers were working in factories and other businesses.

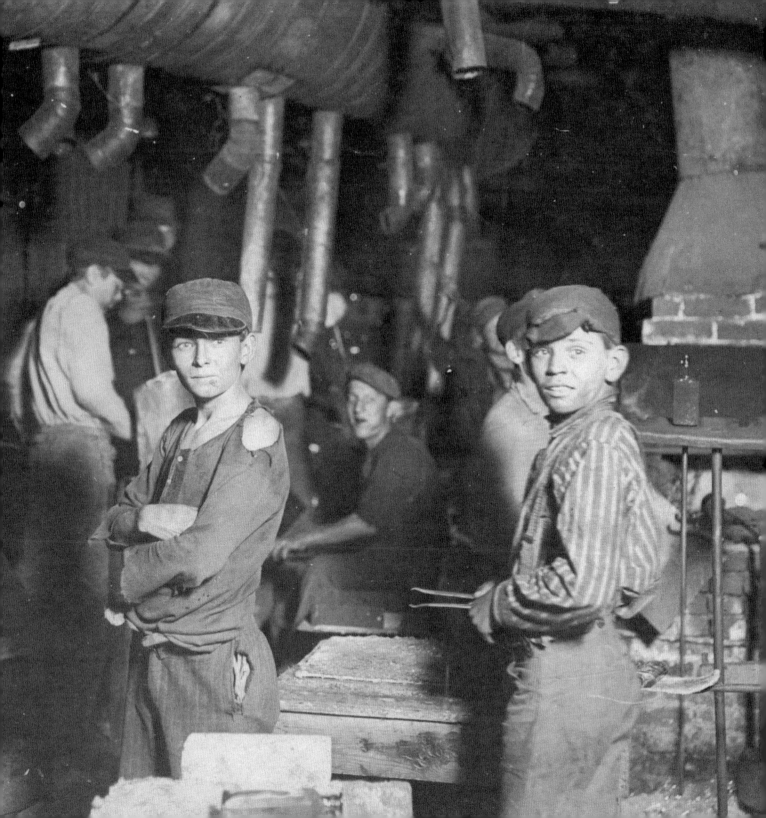

It wasn't until the early 1900s when regulations and laws were passed to ensure the safety and health of children and limit the age when they could be hired and the hours they could work.

Now that you've read about life before child labor laws, you may want to read more about the Industrial Revolution in the Baby Professor book Industrial Revolution: The Rise of Machines (Technology and Inventions).

Visit

BABY PROFESSOR
EDUCATION KIDS

www.BabyProfessorBooks.com

to download Free Baby Professor eBooks
and view our catalog of new and exciting
Children's Books

Made in the USA
Monee, IL
12 February 2024

53390427R00040